Table of Contents

List of Figures

List of Tables

Country Acronyms

AUS	Australia
AUT	Austria
BEL	Belgium
BGR	Bulgaria
BRA	Brazil
CAN	Canada
CHN	China
CYP	Cyprus
CZE	Czech Republic
DEU	Germany
DNK	Denmark
ESP	Spain
EST	Estionia
FIN	Finland
FRA	France
GBR	United Kingdom
GRC	Greece
HUN	Hungary
IDN	Indonesia
IND	India
IRL	Ireland
ITA	Italy
JPN	Japan
KOR	Korea
LTU	Lithuania
LUX	Luxembourg
LVA	Latvia
MEX	Mexico
MLT	Malta
NLD	Netherlands
POL	Poland
PRT	Portugal
ROU	Romania
RUS	Russia
SVK	Slovak Republic
SVN	Slovenia
SWE	Sweden
TUR	Turkey
TWN	Taiwan
USA	United States

1 Introduction

1.1 Background

As national manufacturing supply chains migrate into an integrated global system, there is concern that U.S. manufacturing is being hollowed out. Hollowing out occurs when intermediate goods and services for manufacturing are imported rather than produced domestically, resulting in a loss of other economic assets/activities.[1,2,3] These items may be imported from an overseas company or a U.S. company that has moved production and/or services overseas. There are a number of factors that impact factory location decisions, including cost factors, labor productivity, government stability, infrastructure, and supply chain factors among others.[4]

Statistical, mathematical, and empirical evidence for the hollowing out of the U.S. supply chain is somewhat unclear, as data challenges make it difficult to conduct thorough analyses of such issues.[5] Many studies point to the increased value of imported supply chain goods and services; however, this does not create a complete image, as it does not provide a comparison to other nations. If other countries are importing their supply chain at a similar rate as the U.S., then, it might be that national economies are becoming more globally integrated rather than a trend where the U.S. is losing its manufacturing activity to its international competitors.

Despite competition from abroad, the U.S. is still a major manufacturer. In 2010, the U.S. produced approximately 18 % of the world's manufactured goods, and was the second largest manufacturing nation, down from being the largest in 2009, according to United Nations Statistics Division (UNSD) data. Although, while many products are assembled offshore, semiconductors and other components along with software are developed in the U.S.[6] The manufacturing industry is indispensable to the U.S. economy, as it affects 28 % of U.S. output;[7] however, numerous media articles and some industry experts have discussed the decline of U.S. manufacturing with many proposing that the U.S. has lost its competitive edge.[8] There is also a concern that the hollowing out of domestic

---

[1] Tassey Gregory. "Rationales and Mechanisms for Revitalizing U.S. Manufacturing R&D Strategies." *Journal of Technology Transfer*. 35 (2010): 283-333.

[2] Pisano, Gary P. and Willy C. Shih. Restoring American Competitiveness. *Harvard Business Review*. July-August (2009).

[3] Levinson, Marc. "Hollowing Out in U.S. Manufacturing: Analysis and Issues for Congress." Congressional Research Service. 7-5700. R41712. (2013).

[4] Bhatnagar, Rohit and Amrik S. Sohal. "Supply Chain Competitiveness: Measureing the Impact of Location Factors, Uncertainty and Manufacturing Practices." Technovation. 25 (2005): 443-456.

[5] Levinson, Marc. "Hollowing Out in U.S. Manufacturing: Analysis and Issues for Congress." Congressional Research Service. 7-5700. R41712. (2013).

[6] Duhigg, Charles and Keith Bradsher. "How the U.S. Lost out on iPhone Work." New York Times. January 21, 2012. <http://www nytimes.com/2012/01/22/business/apple-america-and-a-squeezed-middle-class.html?_r=4&pagewanted=all&>

[7] OECD. (2013) StatExtracts. http://stats.oecd.org/Index.aspx. Accessed May 2013

[8] Sirkin, Harold L. Made in the USA Still Means Something. Bloomberg Businessweek. 2009. http://www.businessweek.com/managing/content/apr2009/ca20090410_054122 htm.

manufacturing may negatively affect industry growth potential. It has been suggested that knowledge supporting emerging technologies involves person-to-person contact for efficient transfer; therefore, co-location synergies are important.[9] As supply chains are increasingly imported, this interaction can be diminished, resulting in a loss of research and development and the associated technological knowledge. Manufacturing accounts for a majority of research and development in the U.S. and the loss of this activity is likely to affect growth in both manufacturing and high-tech services.

1.2 Purpose

The purpose of this report is to examine the extent that the U.S. supply chain is being relocated offshore. Specifically, it develops a quantitative depiction of the U.S. manufacturing supply chain in the context of international supply chains. The report analyzes the U.S. manufacturing supply chain and compares it to supply chains of its international counterparts such as trading partners and those countries that are often considered as competitors.

1.3 Scope and Approach

Although national economies are commonly compared to companies competing for market share, this type of analogy provides limited insight and is, unfortunately, rather misleading.[10, 11, 12, 13, 14] A national economy is the primary supplier of goods and services to its labor force while a single company, generally, is not the primary supplier of goods and services to its employees. Additionally, a national economy provides the income for the majority of the nation's consumers while a business, generally, does not provide the income for the majority of its customers. Moreover, a national economy represents a system of exchange in which a company operates as one entity of that system. Companies can go out of business while nations do not. Domestic demand for goods and services constitutes a great proportion of the demand for a nation's domestically-produced products whereas the demand for goods and services from a

---

[9] Tassey Gregory. "Rationales and Mechanisms for Revitalizing U.S. Manufacturing R&D Strategies." *Journal of Technology Transfer*. 35 (2010): 283-333.

[10] Krugman, Paul R. "Making Sense of the Competitiveness Debate." Oxford Review of Economic Policy. Vol 12, no. 3 (1996): 17-25. Paul Krugman won the 2008 Nobel Memorial Prize in Economic Sciences for his work on international trade and economic geography.

[11] Krugman, Paul R. "Competitiveness, A Dangerous Obsession." *Foreign Affairs*. Vol 73. Num 2. March/April (1994): 28-44.

[12] The World Economic Forum defines competitiveness of a nation as "the set of institutions, policies, and factors that determine the level of productivity of a country." This definition relates to productivity and is not consistent with the idea of countries competing for market share. World Economic Forum. *The Global Competitiveness Report*. 2010-2011.
<http://www3.weforum.org/docs/WEF_GlobalCompetitivenessReport_2010-11.pdf>

[13] Porter, Michael E. *The Competitive Advantage of Nations*. 1st ed. (New York: The Free Press, 1990).

[14] Porter asserts that competitiveness is measured by productivity and that measuring a country's competitiveness as its share of world markets is "deeply flawed." Porter, Michael E. "Building the Microeconomic Foundations of Prosperity: Findings from the Business Competitiveness Index." In Porter, Michael E., Klaus Schwab, Xavier Sala-i-Martin, and Augusta Lopez-Claros. The Global Competitiveness Report 2003-2004. (New York: Oxford University Press, 2004).

company is primarily external. This realization has implications for developing an approach to examine the U.S. supply chain, as some approaches provide productive insight while others do not. For example, one might examine the temporal changes in the percent of U.S. supplier value added as a percent of global supplier value added (i.e., U.S. market share of the supply chain); however, the conclusions that can be drawn from this type of analysis are limited. In order for underdeveloped countries to become developed countries, their production and income will need to approach that of the developed world. This, inevitably, results in a decline in the proportion or market share that each developed country represents.

In addition to countries being compared to companies, frequently, anecdotal observations are used to characterize the manufacturing industry;[15] however, the insight from these types of observations is somewhat limited, as the manufacturing industry includes hundreds of thousands of establishments with millions of employees making trillions of dollars' worth of goods. Anecdotal observations provide a limited narrow scope of the industry that does not necessarily reflect or apply to the industry as a whole; thus, this report will largely avoid using these types of comparisons and anecdotes as evidence for economic trends. This approach reduces the possibility of mischaracterizing the industry and provides an evidence-based depiction of the manufacturing industry and its subsectors.

This report uses input-output data from the World Input-Output Database to track the intermediate goods and services used in national manufacturing industries. Specifically, it examines the extent that supply chains are imported and the extent that this trend has changed for the U.S. and other countries. The U.S. data is compared to 39 other countries between 1995 and 2009, a 15 year period. Throughout the report there are discussions about imported goods and services. It is important to note that these are imports of intermediate goods and services used by the manufacturing industry and not the import of final goods and services for other industries or for end use.

---

[15] Greenwald, Bruce C.N. and Judd Kahn. Globalization: The Irrational Fear that Someone in China will Take Your Job. (Hoboken, NJ: John Wiley & Sons 2009).

2 Manufacturing Value Chain

This analysis utilizes the World Input-Output Database (WIOD), which provides data for 40 countries between 1995 and 2009. These countries represented approximately 88 % of manufacturing value added in 2009, according to United Nations data.[16] The data covers 35 industries categorized using the International Standards Industrial Classification (rev. 2) system (see Table 2.1).[17] Input-output data describes the sales and purchases of

Table 2.1: World Input-Output Database Characteristics

Countries Covered			Industries Covered	
1	AUS	Australia	1	Agriculture, Hunting, Forestry and Fishing
2	AUT	Austria	2	Mining and Quarrying
3	BEL	Belgium	3	Food, Beverages and Tobacco
4	BGR	Bulgaria	4	Textiles and Textile Products
5	BRA	Brazil	5	Leather, Leather and Footwear
6	CAN	Canada	6	Wood and Products of Wood and Cork
7	CHN	China	7	Pulp, Paper, Paper , Printing and Publishing
8	CYP	Cyprus	8	Coke, Refined Petroleum and Nuclear Fuel
9	CZE	Czech Republic	9	Chemicals and Chemical Products
10	DNK	Denmark	10	Rubber and Plastics
11	ESP	Spain	11	Other Non-Metallic Mineral
12	EST	Estonia	12	Basic Metals and Fabricated Metal
13	FIN	Finland	13	Machinery (not elsewhere classified)
14	FRA	France	14	Electrical and Optical Equipment
15	GBR	United Kingdom	15	Transport Equipment
16	DEU	Germany	16	Manufacturing not elsewhere classified; Recycling
17	GRC	Greece	17	Electricity, Gas and Water Supply
18	HUN	Hungary	18	Construction
19	IDN	Indonesia	19	Sale, Maintenance and Repair of Motor Vehicles and Motorcycles; Retail Sale of Fuel
20	IND	India	20	Wholesale Trade and Commission Trade, Except of Motor Vehicles and Motorcycles
21	IRL	Ireland	21	Retail Trade, Except of Motor Vehicles and Motorcycles; Repair of Household Goods
22	ITA	Italy	22	Hotels and Restaurants
23	JPN	Japan	23	Inland Transport
24	KOR	Korea	24	Water Transport
25	LTU	Lithuania	25	Air Transport
26	LUX	Luxembourg	26	Other Supporting and Auxiliary Transport Activities; Activities of Travel Agencies
27	LVA	Latvia	27	Post and Telecommunications
28	MEX	Mexico	28	Financial Intermediation
29	MLT	Malta	29	Real Estate Activities
30	NLD	Netherlands	30	Renting of M&Eq and Other Business Activities
31	POL	Poland	31	Public Admin and Defence; Compulsory Social Security
32	PRT	Portugal	32	Education
33	ROU	Romania	33	Health and Social Work
34	RUS	Russia	34	Other Community, Social and Personal Services
35	SVK	Slovak Republic	35	Private Households with Employed Persons
36	SVN	Slovenia		
37	SWE	Sweden		
38	TUR	Turkey		
39	TWN	Taiwan		
40	USA	United States		

[16] United Nations Statistics Division. "National Accounts Main Aggregates Database." <http://unstats.un.org/unsd/snaama/Introduction.asp>

[17] Timmer, Marcel. The World Input-Output Database (WIOD): Contents, Sources, and Methods. April 2012, version 0.9. <http://www.wiod.org/publications/source_docs/WIOD_sources.pdf>

final and intermediate goods and services within an economy. The WIOD tracks intermediate goods and services by industry by country, making it possible to ascertain the proportion of each country's manufacturing supply chain that is imported and to examine other relevant factors. It is important to note that the following analyses do not examine final goods and services imported into a nation, as it focuses on the suppliers to manufacturing.

For this examination, entities involved in the manufacturing supply chain are broken into six categories:

1. Domestic manufacturers
2. Foreign manufacturers
3. Domestic suppliers of manufactured goods
4. Domestic suppliers of non-manufactured goods and services
5. Foreign suppliers of manufactured goods
6. Foreign suppliers of non-manufactured goods and services

Examining the extent to which U.S. manufacturing is being hollowed out requires examining the extent that foreign suppliers (i.e., entities 5 and 6) to domestic manufacturing (i.e., entity 1) are replacing domestic suppliers (i.e., entities 3 and 4). Typically, value added is the best measure available for comparing the relative economic importance of manufacturing activities. The World Input-Output Database defines it as the compensation for labor and capital services.[18] More generally, value added is the sum of compensation, gross operating surplus, and taxes. Input-output data is collected in terms of output; thus, value added is estimated from this data. In recent years there has been concern about the precision of some measures of value added over time. Particularly, there is concern about the use of chained dollars, as discussed by Atkinson.[19] This report uses the producer price index when activity is traced over time, which avoids the issue regarding chained value added. When tracking manufacturing value added over time using the producer price index, it shows a decline of 9.8% between 2000 and 2009, which is consistent with Atkinson's findings. Thus, the measurement problems of chained GDP are not an issue in the measurement of U.S. manufacturing value added in this study.

The value added for the U.S. manufacturing industry and its supply chain is presented in Figure 2.1. The values at the top, shown in red, represent value added that is imported to the U.S. for use by the manufacturing industry. The top value, shown in a lighter red, represents intermediate imported non-manufactured goods and services, such as raw materials from mining. The second one, shown in a darker red, represents intermediate imported manufactured goods used by the U.S. manufacturing industry. Domestic U.S. manufacturing activity is shown in three shades of blue. The light blue represents

---

[18] Timmer, Marcel. The World Input-Output Database (WIOD): Contents, Sources, and Methods. April 2012, version 0.9. <http://www.wiod.org/publications/source_docs/WIOD_sources.pdf>

[19] Atkinson, Robert D., Luke A. Stewart, Scott M. Andes, and Stephen J. Ezell. "Worse than the Great Depression: What Experts are Missing about American Manufacturing Decline." <http://www2.itif.org/2012-american-manufacturing-decline.pdf>

Figure 2.1: U.S. Manufacturing and Supply Chain Value Added

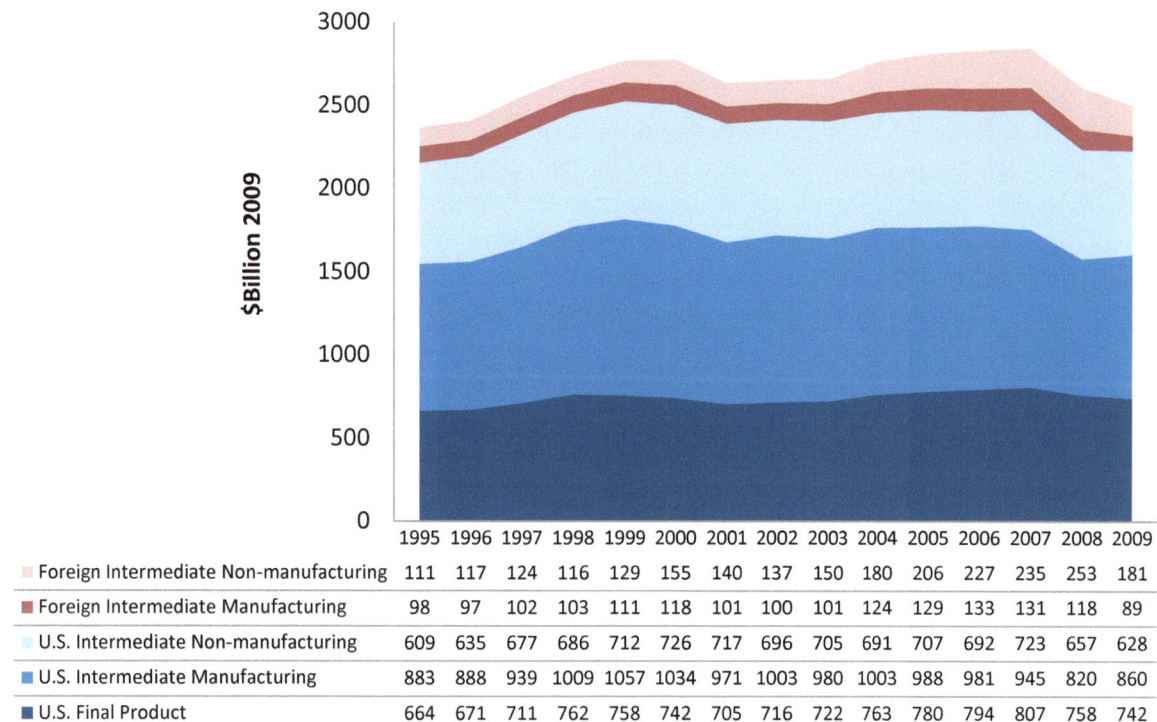

	1995	1996	1997	1998	1999	2000	2001	2002	2003	2004	2005	2006	2007	2008	2009
Foreign Intermediate Non-manufacturing	111	117	124	116	129	155	140	137	150	180	206	227	235	253	181
Foreign Intermediate Manufacturing	98	97	102	103	111	118	101	100	101	124	129	133	131	118	89
U.S. Intermediate Non-manufacturing	609	635	677	686	712	726	717	696	705	691	707	692	723	657	628
U.S. Intermediate Manufacturing	883	888	939	1009	1057	1034	971	1003	980	1003	988	981	945	820	860
U.S. Final Product	664	671	711	762	758	742	705	716	722	763	780	794	807	758	742

intermediate non-manufactured goods and services, such as agricultural products or finance products, produced in the U.S. and used by the U.S. manufacturing industry. The darker blue represents intermediate manufactured products used by the U.S. manufacturing industry; for example, a bolt used to assemble a car. The bottom value, shown in a dark blue, represents final products manufactured in the U.S. As can be seen in the figure, the imported values are a relatively small percentage of the total activity.

Figure 2.2 presents the intermediate imported value added as a percent of U.S. manufactured final product valued added plus intermediate value added. That is, the figure presents intermediate imported value added used by a nation's manufacturing industry as a percent of all value added associated with that nation's manufacturing industry. For example, for the U.S. it would be the values shown in red from Figure 2.1 divided by all the values shown in red and blue in the figure and calculated for each year. For all products produced in a particular country, it represents the percent that does not originate from that country. In 2009, the U.S. imported 10.8 % of its supply chain, the 3rd lowest percentage, meaning that in relation to other countries, the U.S. imports a smaller proportion of its supply chain for manufacturing. Between 1995 and 2009, the percentage of imported supply chain value added increased for 32 of the 40 countries examined and for the U.S. it increased by 1.96 percentage points. The average increase for the 32 countries was 4.67 percentage points and the average change for all countries was an increase of 2.78 percentage points; thus, the U.S. percentage increase in supply chain imports is slightly below the average. China increased by 4.92 percentage points while

Japan increased by 4.59 percentage points. The U.S. peaked in 2008 at 14.2 % and ranked as the 6th lowest at that time.

Figure 2.3 presents intermediate imported value added as a percent of national manufacturing supply chain value added (i.e., intermediate value added). It represents the percent of the nation's supply chain for manufacturing that is imported. For example, for the U.S. it would be the two values in red from Figure 2.1 divided by the sum of the two values shown in red and the values for the two lighter shades of blue. With a 2009 value of 15.4 % and ranking as the 4th lowest, the U.S. imports a smaller proportion of its supply chain compared to other countries; however, it is important to note that the size of an economy and its manufacturing industry correlate negatively with the proportion of its supply chain that is imported, as illustrated in Figure 2.4. Therefore, a country with a larger manufacturing industry and/or larger economy would be expected to import a smaller proportion of its supply chain. Figure 2.2 and Figure 2.3 confirm that the U.S. is among the lowest as would be expected of a large economy. Additionally, the U.S. proportion has not grown as fast as many other countries. Between 1995 and 2009, the U.S. percentage increased as did that for 33 other countries out of the 40 total. For the 34 countries with increases, the average increase was 6.55 percentage points while the U.S. increased by 3.07 percentage points. Germany, China, and India grew by 8.75, 7.24, and 8.32 percentage points. The average change for all countries was an increase of 4.94 percentage points; thus, the U.S. was slightly below average. Figure 2.5 presents data for 1995 and 2009 imported intermediate manufacturing value added as a percent of national manufacturing supply chain value added (i.e., the two end points in Figure 2.3). Those countries that are above the dashed 45 degree line saw their percentage increase in value while those below it saw it decrease. Among those that decreased are Indonesia, Russia, Canada, Cyprus, Estonia, and Malta.

As discussed previously, hollowing out occurs when 1) intermediate goods and services for manufacturing are increasingly imported rather than produced domestically and 2) these imported goods result in the loss of other economic assets/activities. Figure 2.2 and Figure 2.3 confirm that foreign suppliers have replaced domestic suppliers in the U.S.; however, it does not confirm that these changes have resulted in a loss of other economic assets/activities. Therefore, increasingly imported intermediate goods and services suggest that some hollowing out may be occurring, but it is not conclusive evidence. Alternatively, increases in imported intermediate goods may be the result of the specialization in the production of goods, where resources are transferred from one sector to another. This trend could result in importing goods that are not within the area of specialization.

It is important to note the difference between Figure 2.2 and Figure 2.3. The former shows a nation's supply chain in terms of the intermediate and final goods and services associated with manufactured products while the later shows it in terms of the intermediate goods and services. Distinguishing between an entity in a nation that supplies manufactured goods to that nation's manufacturing industry from an entity that produces final goods is somewhat arbitrary. Typically, data is distinguished by establishment, which is a single physical location where manufacturing is conducted and

Figure 2.2: Intermediate Imported Value Added for Manufacturing as a Percent of Final Product Value Added Plus all Intermediate Value Added

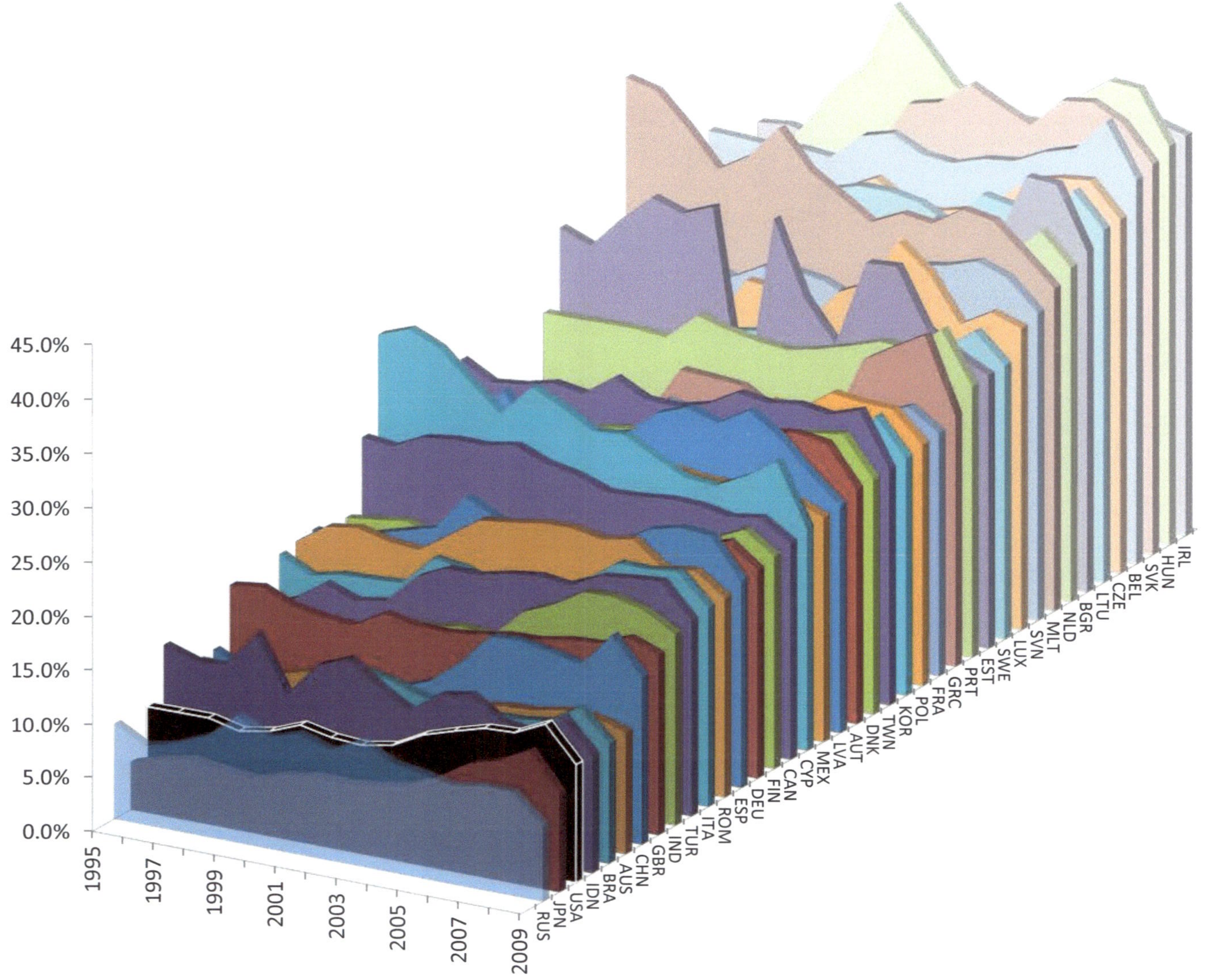

Figure 2.3: Intermediate Imported Value Added for Manufacturing as a Percent of Intermediate Value Added

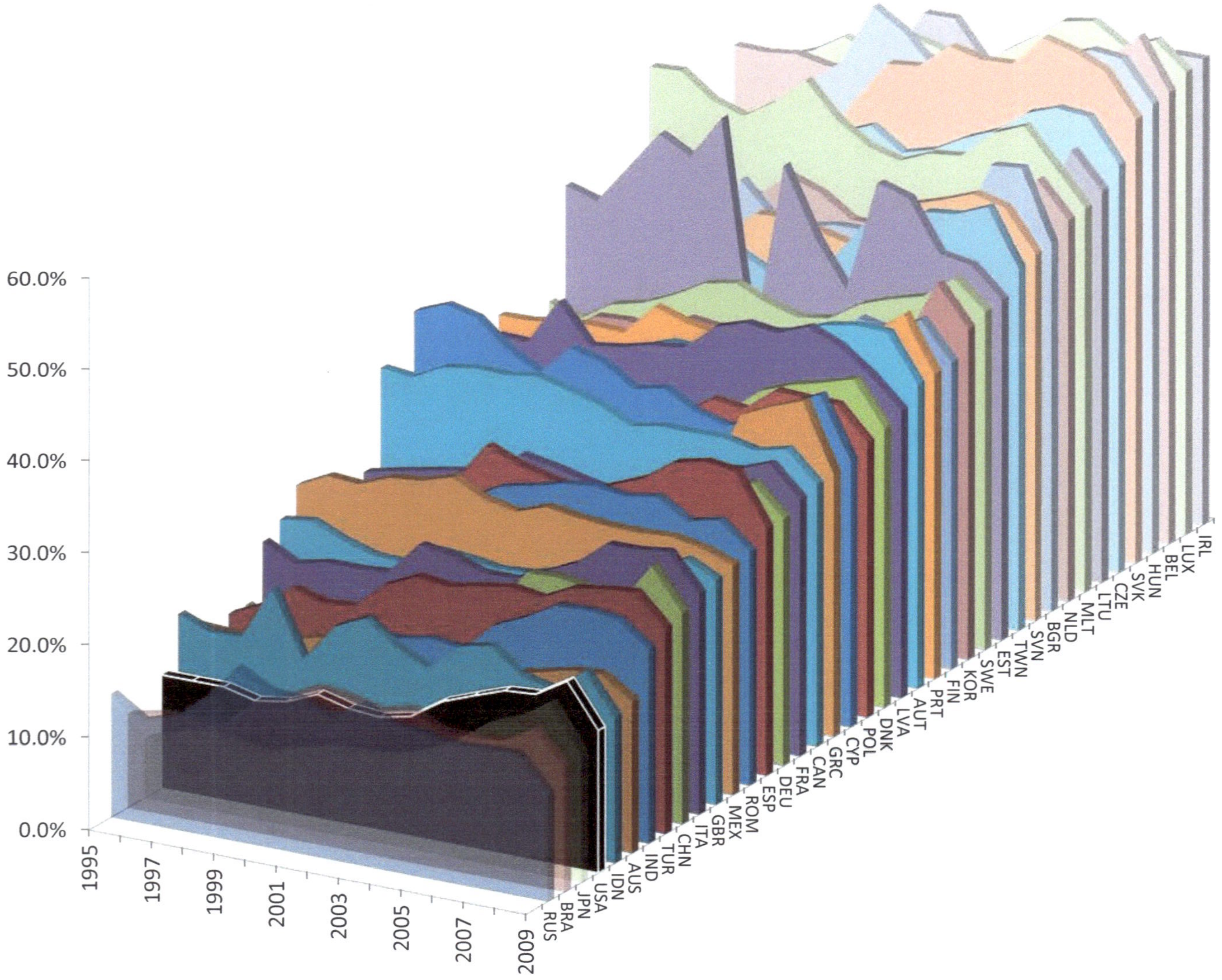

Figure 2.4: Intermediate Imported Value Added for Manufacturing as a Percent of Final Product Value Added Plus all Intermediate Value Added, 1995-2009

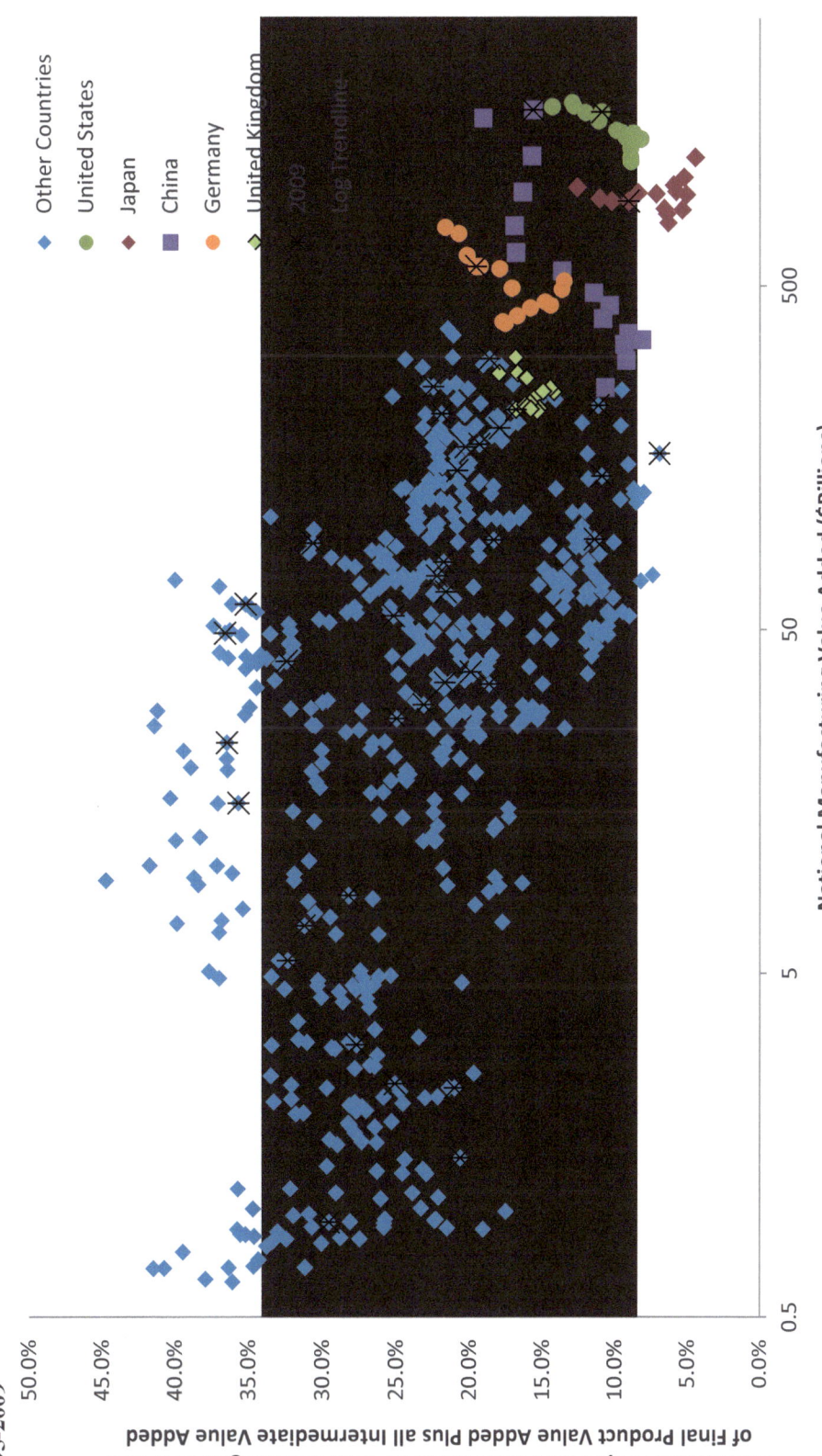

Note: This figure presents data from Figure 2.2 combined with manufacturing value added for the corresponding country.

11

should not be confused with an enterprise or company; thus, it is somewhat arbitrary whether a company produces all of a product in one location or in two locations with one location being a supplier to the other.

Figure 2.2 shows that intermediate imported value added as a percent of final product value added plus intermediate value added in the U.S. increased from 8.8 % in 1995 to a peak of 14.2 % in 2008, a 61 % increase in the percentage; however, it still remains well below that of many other nations. Figure 2.3 shows that the U.S. supply chain is increasingly relying on imports; however, it still remains a smaller proportion than many other countries.

U.S. final product value added grew by 21.6 % between 1995 and the peak of final product value added in 2007, as seen in Figure 2.1. Meanwhile, domestically produced supply chain value added increased 11.8 %. During the same period, foreign-produced supply chain value added grew 74.7 %. It is important to note that foreign activity may be replacing both domestic supply chains and manufacturing activity itself, as there is a trend where manufacturing activities are being unbundled into other industries. For instance, at one time a company might have had its own staff to handle tax preparations, whereas today, it might outsource these activities to a company that specializes in tax preparation. This causes activities previously categorized as part of the manufacturing industry to be categorized under a different industry. As can be seen in Figure 2.6, the ratio of the supply chain of non-manufacturing value added to

Figure 2.5: Percent of the Manufacturing Supply Chain that is Imported

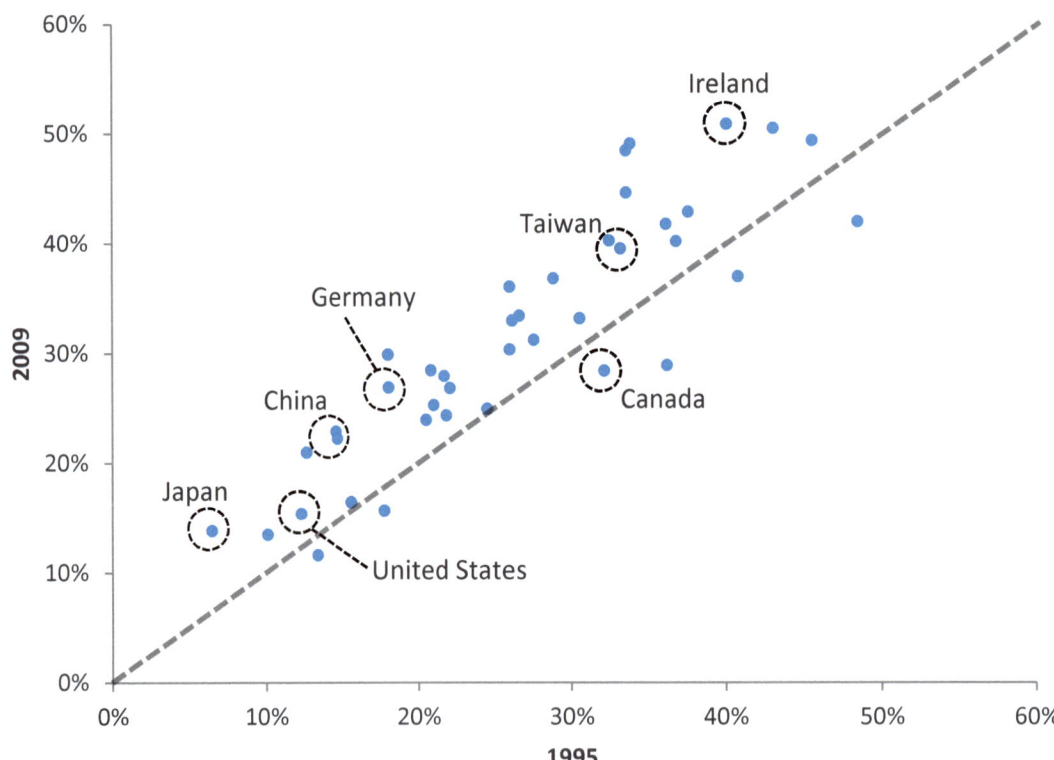

Figure 2.6: Ratio of the Supply Chain of Non-Manufacturing Value Added to Manufacturing Value Added

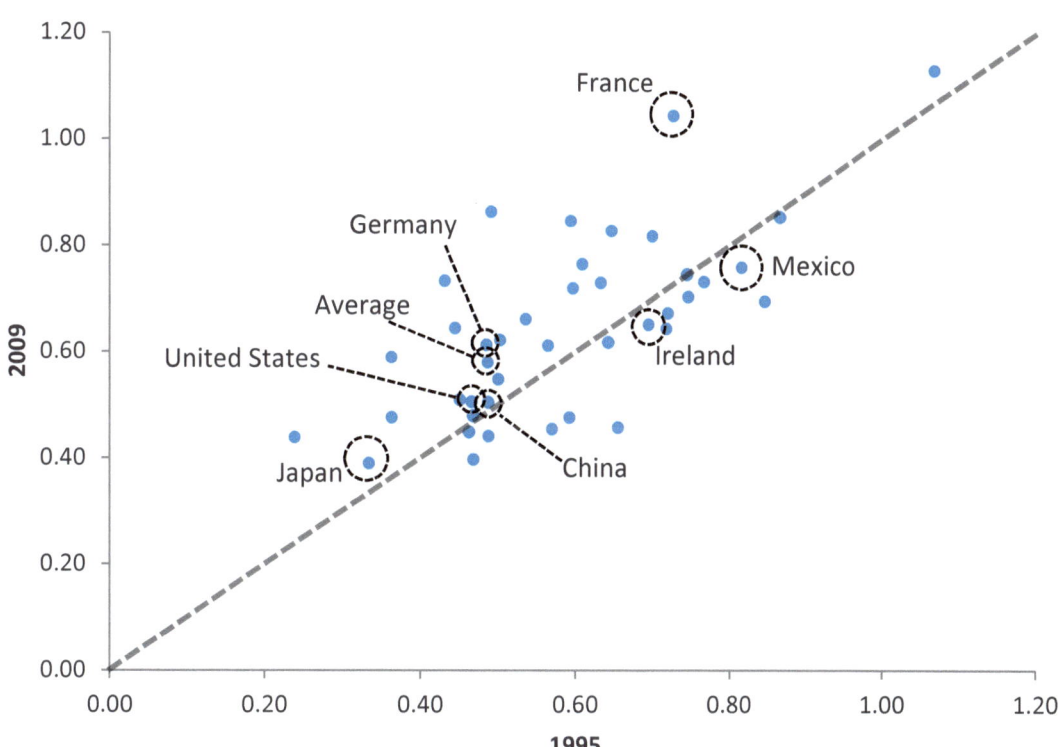

manufacturing value added increased for a number of countries and the average increased from 0.49 to 0.58.

One concern with the hollowing out of U.S. manufacturing is that high-tech activities involving research and development may be moved offshore. Figure 2.7 and Figure 2.8 present the manufacturing supply chain imports in 2009 as a percent of national manufacturing value added and intermediate value added.[20] As seen in Figure 2.7 and Figure 2.8, the highest values for U.S. imports is 44 % for agriculture and mining with the next highest being 21 % for transportation. In all cases, the U.S. was below the average. For instance, of the rental, computer services, and R&D used by the U.S. manufacturing industry, 13 % of it is imported from other countries and is the second lowest. This value is consistent with the fact that the U.S. is among the top science and technology innovators.[21] The percent imported for rental, computer services, and R&D used by the U.S. manufacturing industry increased from 11 % in 1995 to 13 % in 2009, as seen in Figure 2.9. While this value increased for the U.S., it decreased for 21 of the 40 countries examined. For the average of all countries, it decreased by 2.0 % while the U.S. increased by 2.1 %. The correlation coefficient between the change in the percent of the supply chain that is imported (i.e., data from Figure 2.5) and the percent of the supply chain that is imported for rentals, computer services, and R&D (i.e. from Figure 2.9) is

---

[20] Other things being equal, lower values are considered to be favorable to higher values.

[21] Thomas, Douglas. The Current State and Recent Trends of the U.S. Manufacturing Industry. NIST Special Publication 1142. National Institute of Standards and Technology. 2012. <http://nvlpubs.nist.gov/nistpubs/SpecialPublications/NIST.SP.1142.pdf>

13

0.39. Thus, as manufacturing supply chains are increasingly imported, there is a tendency for the proportion of rentals, computer services, and R&D imported to increase. However, the correlation is weak, suggesting that it is either not a major factor or that there are other factors that play a role.

Figure 2.7: Percent of Manufacturing Supply Chain that is Imported, by Industry Categories (2009)

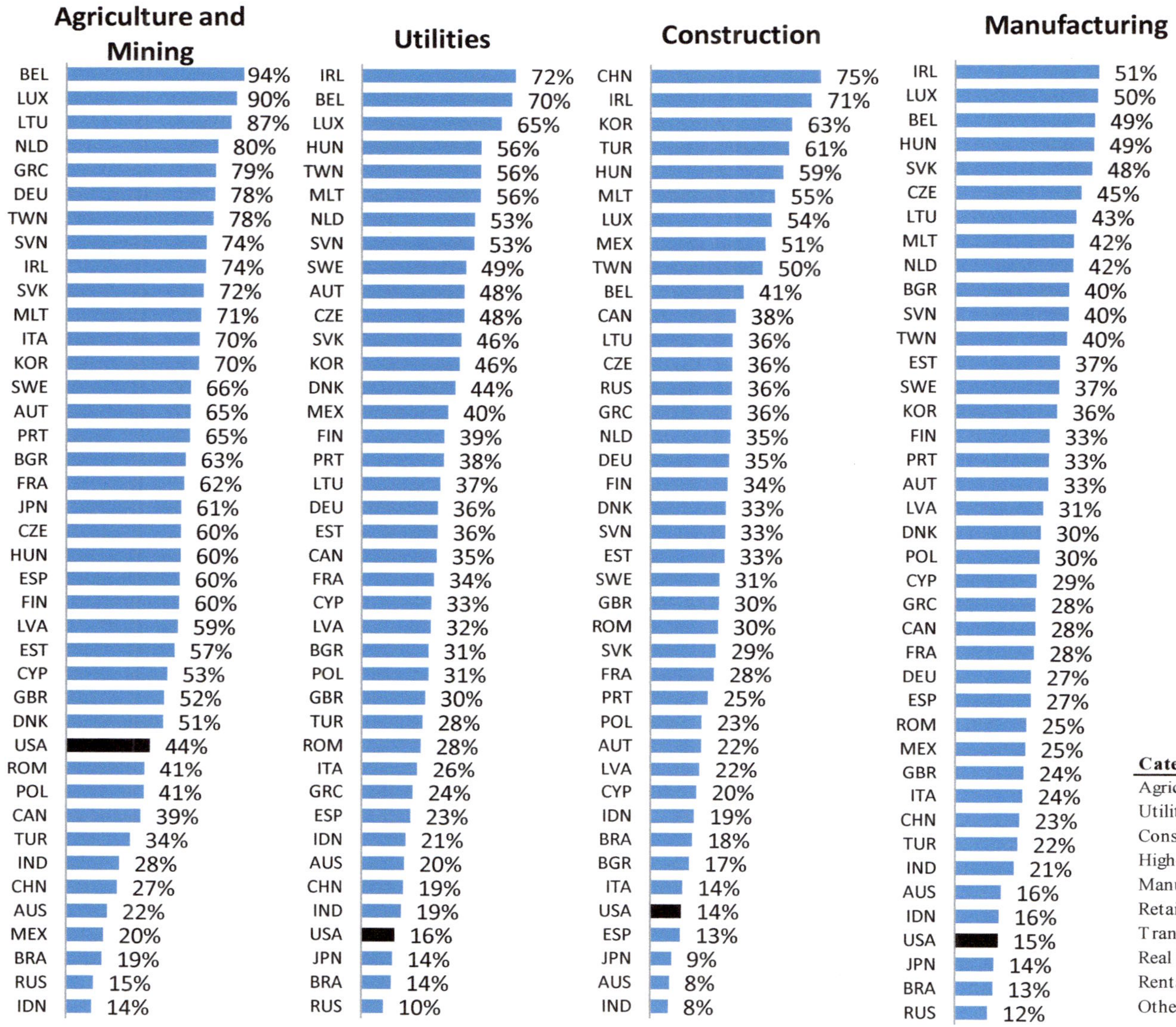

Agriculture and Mining

BEL	94%
LUX	90%
LTU	87%
NLD	80%
GRC	79%
DEU	78%
TWN	78%
SVN	74%
IRL	74%
SVK	72%
MLT	71%
ITA	70%
KOR	70%
SWE	66%
AUT	65%
PRT	65%
BGR	63%
FRA	62%
JPN	61%
CZE	60%
HUN	60%
ESP	60%
FIN	60%
LVA	59%
EST	57%
CYP	53%
GBR	52%
DNK	51%
USA	44%
ROM	41%
POL	41%
CAN	39%
TUR	34%
IND	28%
CHN	27%
AUS	22%
MEX	20%
BRA	19%
RUS	15%
IDN	14%

Utilities

IRL	72%
BEL	70%
LUX	65%
HUN	56%
TWN	56%
MLT	56%
NLD	53%
SVN	53%
SWE	49%
AUT	48%
CZE	48%
SVK	46%
KOR	46%
DNK	44%
MEX	40%
FIN	39%
PRT	38%
LTU	37%
DEU	36%
EST	36%
CAN	35%
FRA	34%
CYP	33%
LVA	32%
BGR	31%
POL	31%
GBR	30%
TUR	28%
ROM	28%
ITA	26%
GRC	24%
ESP	23%
IDN	21%
AUS	20%
CHN	19%
IND	19%
USA	16%
JPN	14%
BRA	14%
RUS	10%

Construction

CHN	75%
IRL	71%
KOR	63%
TUR	61%
HUN	59%
MLT	55%
LUX	55%
MEX	51%
TWN	50%
BEL	41%
CAN	38%
LTU	36%
CZE	36%
RUS	36%
GRC	36%
NLD	35%
DEU	35%
FIN	34%
DNK	33%
SVN	33%
EST	33%
SWE	31%
GBR	30%
ROM	30%
SVK	29%
FRA	28%
PRT	28%
POL	25%
AUT	23%
LVA	22%
CYP	20%
IDN	19%
BRA	18%
BGR	17%
ITA	14%
USA	14%
ESP	13%
JPN	9%
AUS	8%
IND	8%

Manufacturing

IRL	51%
LUX	50%
BEL	49%
HUN	49%
SVK	48%
CZE	45%
LTU	43%
MLT	42%
NLD	42%
BGR	40%
SVN	40%
TWN	40%
EST	37%
SWE	37%
KOR	36%
FIN	33%
PRT	33%
AUT	33%
LVA	31%
DNK	30%
POL	30%
CYP	29%
GRC	28%
CAN	28%
FRA	28%
DEU	27%
ESP	27%
ROM	25%
MEX	25%
GBR	24%
ITA	24%
CHN	23%
TUR	22%
IND	21%
AUS	16%
IDN	16%
USA	15%
JPN	14%
BRA	13%
RUS	12%

Category	ISIC Codes
Agriculture and Mining	1, 2, 5, 10-14
Utilities	64, 40, 41
Construction	45
High-Tech Manufacturing	30, 31, 32, 33
Manufacturing	15-37
Retail and Wholesale Trade	50-52, 55
Transportation	60-63
Real Estate, Finance, and Social Services	65-67, 70, 80, 85, 90-93
Rentals, Computer Services, R&D	71-74
Other	75, 95

15

Figure 2.8: Percent of Manufacturing Supply Chain that is Imported, by Industry Categories (2009)

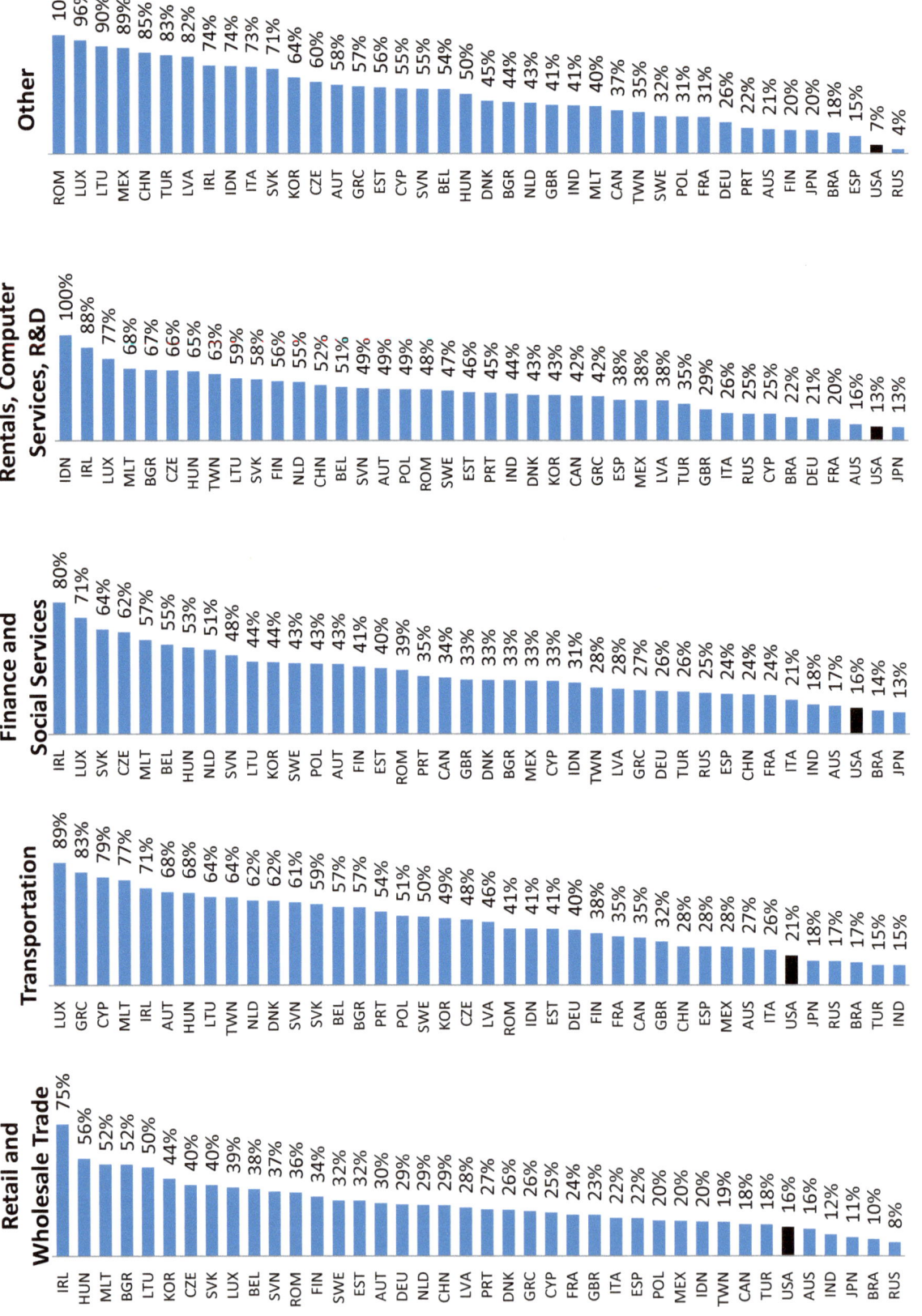

Figure 2.9: Percent of the Manufacturing Supply Chain that is Imported, 1995-2009 (Rentals, Computer Services, R&D)

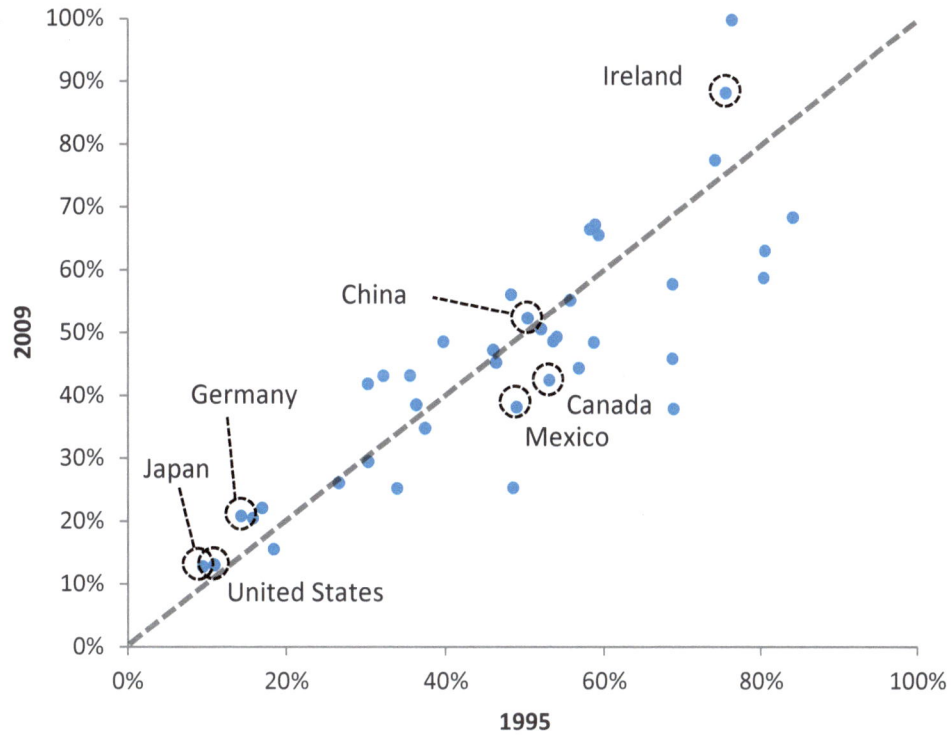

3 Conclusion

This analysis utilized the World Input-Output Database (WIOD), which provides data for 35 industries spanning 40 countries between 1995 and 2009. These countries represented approximately 88 % of manufacturing value added in 2009, according to United Nations data. In terms of 2009 imported supply chain value added used by a nation's manufacturing industry as a percent of all value added associated with that nation's manufacturing industry, the U.S. imported 10.8 % of its supply chain, the 3rd lowest percentage, meaning that in relation to other countries the U.S. imports a smaller proportion of its supply chain for manufacturing. Between 1995 and 2009, the percentage of imported supply chain value added increased for 32 of the 40 countries examined and for the U.S. it increased by 1.96 percentage points. The average increase for the 32 countries was 4.67 percentage points and the average change for all countries was an increase of 2.78 points; thus, the U.S. percentage increase in supply chain imports is slightly below the average. China increased by 4.92 percentage points while Japan increased by 4.59. The U.S. peaked in 2008 at 14.2 % and ranked as the 6th lowest at that time. As a share of the supply chain, the U.S. imported 15.4 % of its supply chain and ranked as the 4th lowest; thus, the U.S. imports a smaller proportion of its supply chain compared to other countries. Between 1995 and 2009, the U.S. percentage increased as did 33 other countries out of the 40 total. For the 34 countries with increases, the average increase was 6.55 percentage points while the U.S. increased by 3.07 percentage points. Germany, China, and India grew by 8.75, 7.24, and 8.32 percentage points. The average change for all countries was an increase of 4.94 percentage points; thus, the U.S. percentage increase in supply chain imports was slightly below the average. These figures confirm that foreign suppliers have replaced some domestic suppliers in the U.S., suggesting that some hollowing may be occurring; however, the increase may also be the result of the specialization in the production of goods.

U.S. final product value added grew by 21.6 % between 1995 and the peak of final product value added in 2007. Meanwhile, domestically produced supply chain value added increased 11.8 %. During the same period, foreign-produced supply chain value added grew 74.7 %. It is important to note that foreign activity may be replacing both domestic supply chains and manufacturing activity itself, as there is a trend where manufacturing activities are being unbundled into other industries.

Literature Cited

Atkinson, Robert D., Luke A. Stewart, Scott M. Andes, and Stephen J. Ezell. "Worse than the Great Depression: What Experts are Missing about American Manufacturing Decline." <http://www2.itif.org/2012-american-manufacturing-decline.pdf>

Bhatnagar, Rohit and Amrik S. Sohal. "Supply Chain Competitiveness: Measureing the Impact of Location Factors, Uncertainty and Manufacturing Practices." Technovation. 25 (2005): 443-456.

Duhigg, Charles and Keith Bradsher. "How the U.S. Lost out on iPhone Work." New York Times. January 21, 2012. <http://www.nytimes.com/2012/01/22/business/apple-america-and-a-squeezed-middle-class.html?_r=4&pagewanted=all&>

Greenwald, Bruce C.N. and Judd Kahn. Globalization: The Irrational Fear that Someone in China will Take Your Job. (Hoboken, NJ: John Wiley & Sons 2009).

Krugman, Paul R. "Competitiveness, A Dangerous Obsession." Foreign Affairs. Vol 73. Num 2. March/April (1994): 28-44.

Krugman, Paul R. "Making Sense of the Competitiveness Debate." Oxford Review of Economic Policy. Vol 12, no. 3 (1996): 17-25.

Levinson, Marc. "Hollowing Out in U.S. Manufacturing: Analysis and Issues for Congress." Congressional Research Service. 7-5700. R41712. (2013).

OECD. (2013) StatExtracts. http://stats.oecd.org/Index.aspx. Accessed May 2013

Pisano, Gary P. and Willy C. Shih. Restoring American Competitiveness. Harvard Business Review. July-August (2009).

Porter, Michael E. "Building the Microeconomic Foundations of Prosperity: Findings from the Business Competitiveness Index." In Porter, Michael E., Klaus Schwab, Xavier Sala-i-Martin, and Augusta Lopez-Claros. The Global Competitiveness Report 2003-2004. (New York: Oxford University Press, 2004).

Porter, Michael E. The Competitive Advantage of Nations. 1st ed. (New York: The Free Press, 1990).

Sirkin, Harold L. Made in the USA Still Means Something. Bloomberg Businessweek. 2009. http://www.businessweek.com/managing/content/apr2009/ca20090410_054122.htm.

Tassey Gregory. "Rationales and Mechanisms for Revitalizing U.S. Manufacturing R&D Strategies." Journal of Technology Transfer. 35 (2010): 283-333.

Thomas, Douglas. The Current State and Recent Trends of the U.S. Manufacturing Industry. NIST Special Publication 1142. National Institute of Standards and Technology. 2012.
<http://nvlpubs.nist.gov/nistpubs/SpecialPublications/NIST.SP.1142.pdf>

Timmer, Marcel. The World Input-Output Database (WIOD): Contents, Sources, and Methods. April 2012, version 0.9.
<http://www.wiod.org/publications/source_docs/WIOD_sources.pdf>

United Nations Statistics Division. 2012. "National Accounts Main Aggregates Database." <http://unstats.un.org/unsd/snaama/Introduction.asp>

World Economic Forum. The Global Competitiveness Report. 2010-2011.
<http://www3.weforum.org/docs/WEF_GlobalCompetitivenessReport_2010-11.pdf>